My Central Line

By Angus Olsen

For Ava.

ISBN: 978-0-6484883-0-9
ABN: 82 796 919 757
https://www.facebook.com/idrawchildhoodcancer/

I have a Central Line,
it is very special and very important.

My Central Line goes inside my chest to where my blood is.

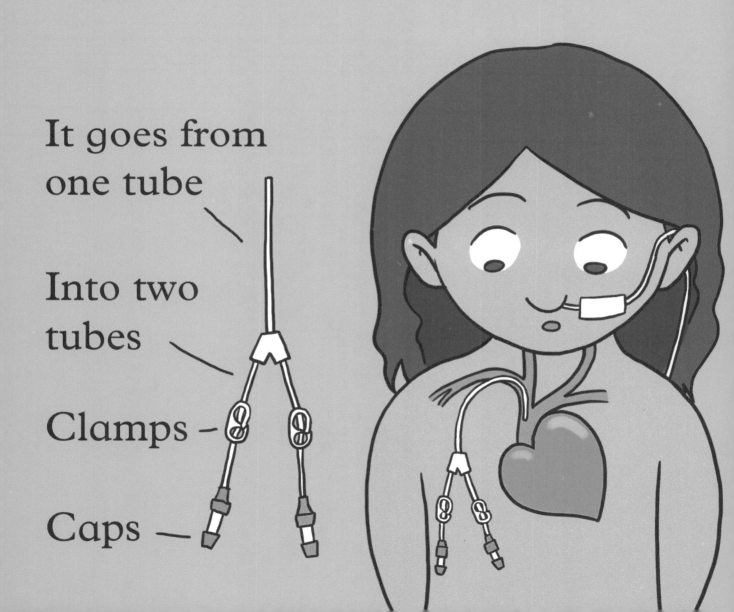

It goes from one tube

Into two tubes

Clamps

Caps

When I have a bath I need to be careful it doesn't go in the water.

They use my Central Line to check my blood.

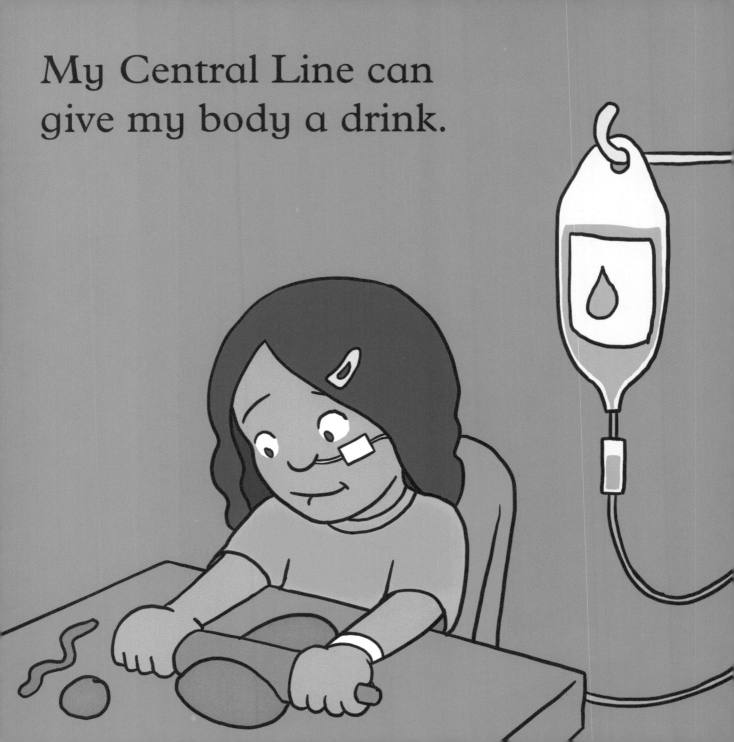

My Central Line can give my body a drink.

My Central Line can give
my body some medicine.

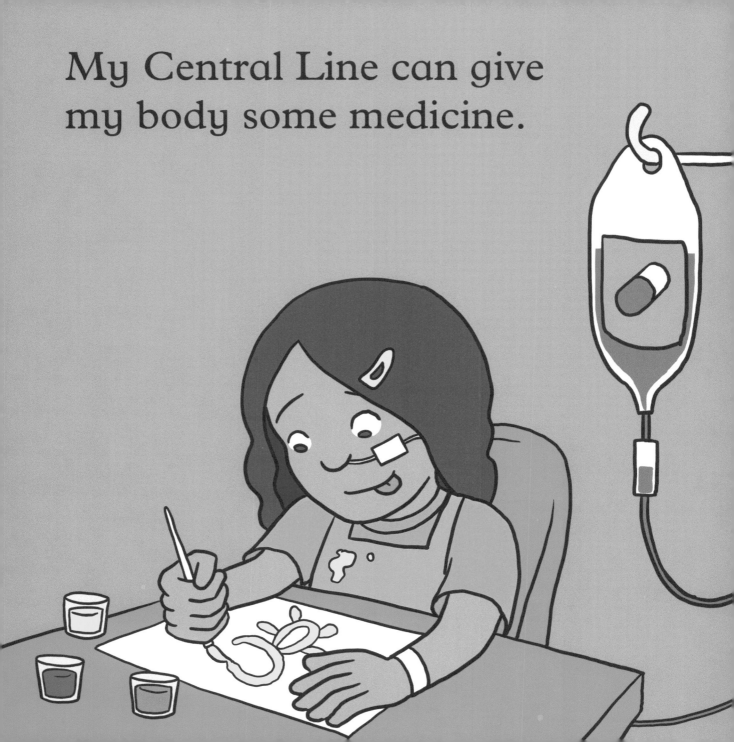

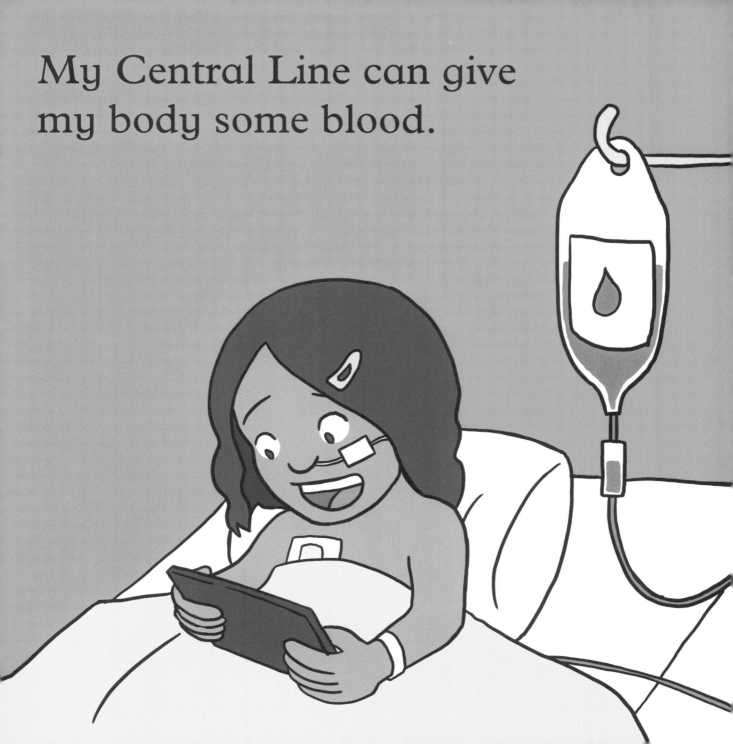

My Central Line can give
my body some blood.

Sometimes my dressing needs changing so it is fresh and clean.

The nurse says
I am very brave.

I have a Central Line, it is very special and very important.

CPSIA information can be obtained
at www.ICGtesting.com
Printed in the USA
LVHW072102230223
740261LV00025B/202